the Sudan PROJECT

Rebuilding With the People of Darfur
A Young Person's Guide

Melissa Leembruggen

Abingdon Press
Nashville

The Sudan Project logo is used with permission from Ginghamsburg United Methodist Church, Tipp City, Ohio. The photographs are used with permission from UMCOR and the photographers. Globe photographed on pp. 4 & 5 © Replogle Globes, Inc. Photos used with their permission.

Photo Credits: front cover, pp. 8, 9, 10, 11, 21, 23, 24 (inset), 25 (bottom) & 26: Paul Jeffrey/UMCOR; pp. 4 & 5: Melissa Leembruggen; pp. 6, 24, 25 (top right), 27, 29 & back cover: Linda Beher/UMCOR; pp. 7 & 12: Sidney Traynham/Ginghamsburg United Methodist Church; p. 13: Michael Treadway/UMCOR; pp. 14, 15, 17 & 28: UMCOR; pp. 16, 18 & 25 (top left): GBGM; pp. 19, 20 & 22: Jane Ohuma/UMCOR, p. 19 (inset): Steven Guy/UMCOR

This book is printed on acid-free paper.

Library of Congress Cataloging-in-Publication Data

Leembruggen, Melissa.
  The Sudan Project : rebuilding with the people of Darfur : a young person's guide / Melissa Leembruggen.
    p. cm.
  ISBN 978-0-687-65050-7 (pbk. : alk. paper)
  1. Refugees–Sudan–Darfur–Juvenile literature. 2. Internally displaced persons–Sudan–Darfur–Juvenile literature. 3. Humanitarian assistance–Sudan–Darfur–Juvenile literature. I. Title.

  HV640.5.S9L44 2007
  962.4043–dc22

                2007021625

07 08 09 10 11 12 13 14 15 16—10 9 8 7 6 5 4 3 2 1
Manufactured in the United States of America

The Dedication

To the children in the Sudan, that someday you will be able to read this book and know that the love of God touched your world.

The History of The Sudan Project

In 1999 Mike Slaughter, Lead Pastor of Ginghamsburg United Methodist Church, was reading the Dayton Daily Newspaper. On one page was an ad for a sedan automobile. On the facing page was an article about children starving in the Sudan. The similarity of the names, and the contrast between affluence and poverty ignited a spark within him. The Holy Spirit of God urged him to look for ways to make a difference in this faraway part of the world.

In 2004, Ginghamsburg Church took the first Christmas Miracle offering and received over $300,000 for relief work in Darfur. They worked with the United Methodist Committee on Relief (UMCOR) to develop a five year plan. They helped create an economy by hiring local workers to produce farm implements. They provided seed money for a sustainable agricultural project. The following harvest season allowed them to feed 25,000 people, provide seed for 5,000 family farms for the next season, and offer extra income for additional family needs.

In 2005, over $500,000 was donated. With this money, a children's protective services program began. Teacher training and skills training for men and women started. Education for both girls (many of whom did not previously have the opportunity to go to school) and boys ensued once the teachers finished training.

In 2006, $1,000,000 arrived at the church from all over the country as word spread about the amazing programs of The Sudan Project. Each year $500,000 is required to sustain the Children's Protective Services program. And the additional $500,000 provides safe, sanitary water yards, which will last 219,000 people and their cattle for many years.

For updates on the activities of The Sudan Project, visit **ginghamsburg.org/sudan**.

The Profits

A percentage of the profits from this book is donated to The Sudan Project, which works in conjunction with UMCOR.

The Purpose

Before coming to Ginghamsburg Church, I was detached from the tragic circumstances of humanity in the Sudan and Africa in general. My brain knew life was hard, but my heart did not want to feel the truth of their lives and the persecution involved. Now my heart has been opened and I am inspired to act in a creative way. Our children are the future leaders of this world. If we help them understand hardship before their hearts are hardened, they will be better leaders for the next generation. This is not just a story to glorify Ginghamsburg Church! It is a story to be shared with the Christian community throughout the world to inspire The Church to action. And it is a story that can help us understand that one person receiving the inspiration of the Holy Spirit and one church using its resources to do God's work can CHANGE the WORLD.

Aa

Africa is the second largest of the seven **continents**.

Africa is south of Europe and is attached to Asia by a small strip of land called the Sinai **Peninsula**. The African continent is bordered by the Mediterranean Sea on the north, the Indian Ocean on the east, the Antarctic Ocean on the south, and the Atlantic Ocean on the west. It has fifty-five countries, the largest of which is the Sudan.

Which continent do you live on?

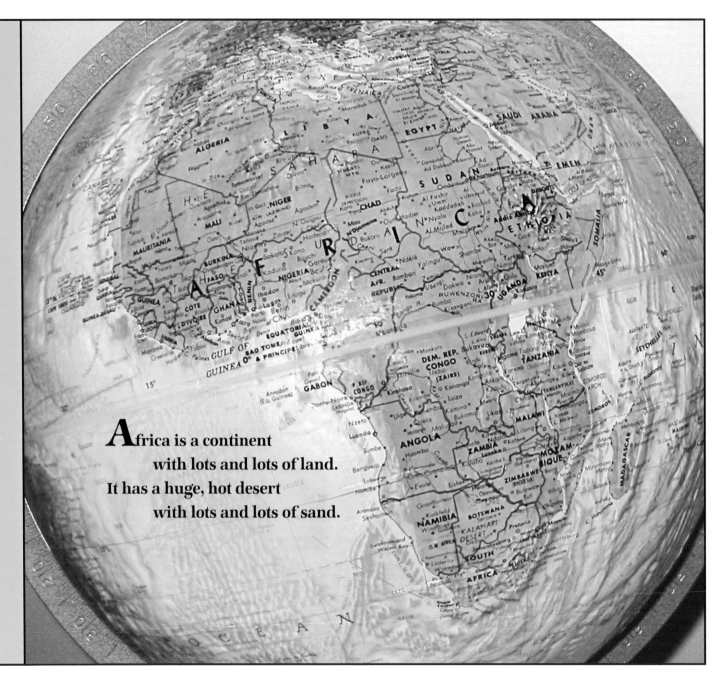

Africa is a continent
with lots and lots of land.
It has a huge, hot desert
with lots and lots of sand.

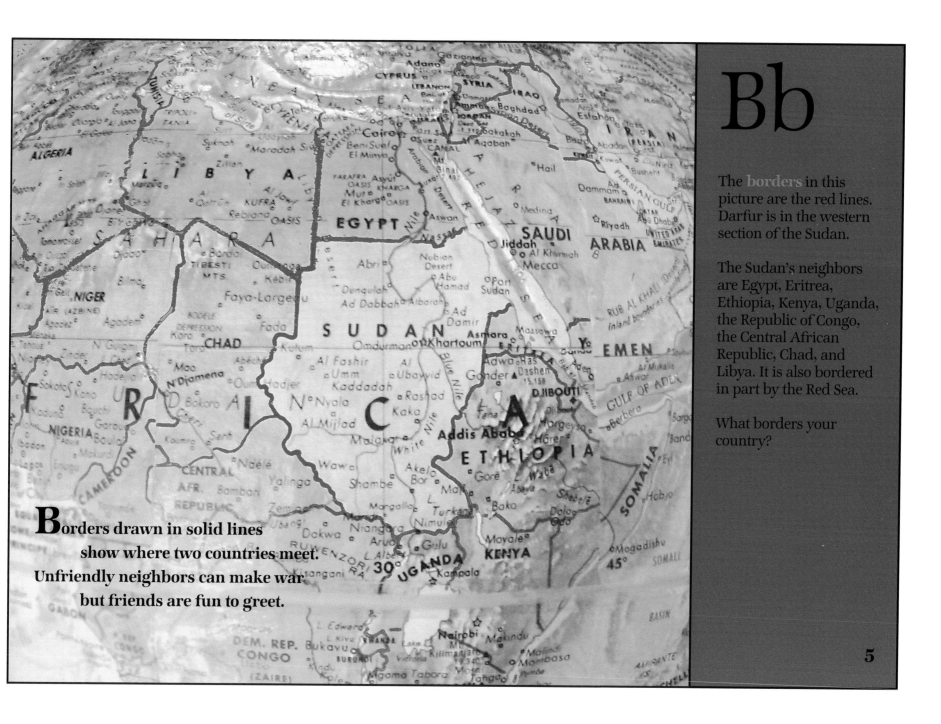

Bb

The **borders** in this picture are the red lines. Darfur is in the western section of the Sudan.

The Sudan's neighbors are Egypt, Eritrea, Ethiopia, Kenya, Uganda, the Republic of Congo, the Central African Republic, Chad, and Libya. It is also bordered in part by the Red Sea.

What borders your country?

Borders drawn in solid lines
   show where two countries meet.
Unfriendly neighbors can make war
   but friends are fun to greet.

Cc

After the great flood mentioned in the Bible in Genesis, Noah's son Ham is said to have traveled to Africa to settle. Ham's oldest son was named Cush.

Cush was a very large area, and part of ancient Cush has become known as the Republic of Sudan.

Where are your **ancestors** from originally?

Cush is a mighty land
of Biblical **acclaim**.
The Republic of Sudan
is now its modern name.

Dd

Darfur is made of three small states
and found in West Sudan.
Lots of people have no homes;
they're hungry in this land.

The Darfur region is made up of three states: Gharb Darfur, Shamal Darfur, and Janub Darfur. The name Darfur means home (dar) of the Fur. The Fur is a group of people that lives in the area.

Ee

A **displaced** person's camp is a temporary village with some basic food, an attempt at clean water, and a small amount of safety. Those people who leave the camp are often caught in the violence from the war. Sometimes with extra help from people who care in other parts of the world, a school, a hospital, a church, or an **orphanage** might be created in a camp to help meet the needs of the men, women, and children who are trying to survive in Darfur.

The tarps on this home help keep the rain out, and the woven mat on the floor makes it less muddy inside.

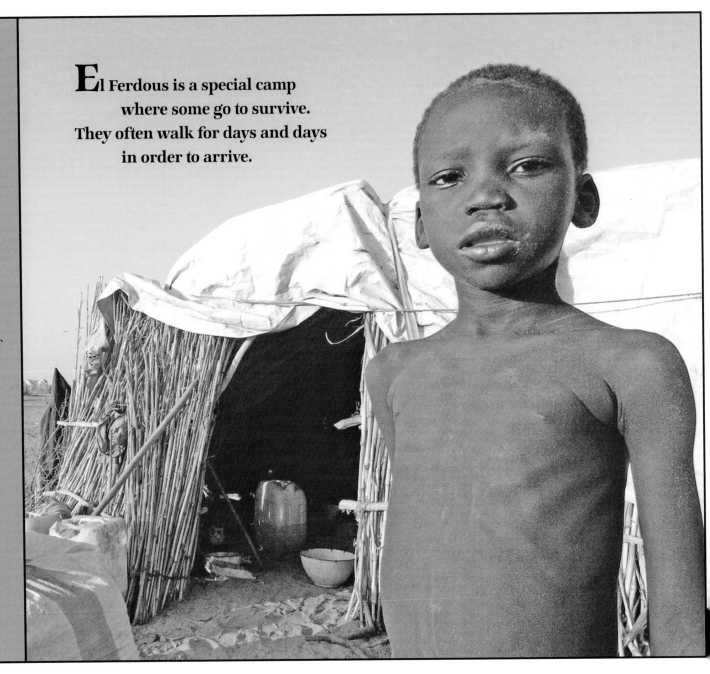

El Ferdous is a special camp where some go to survive. They often walk for days and days in order to arrive.

Farming is a source of life
for families in Sudan.
**The work is hard when tilling soil
is mostly done by hand.**

Ff

Not all of Africa is desert. Africa has jungles, forests, and mountains!

The ground around Darfur is good for farming. Crops provide food that families can eat and cash that they can earn by selling the extra at local markets. When several villagers farm different crops, there is a good nutritional balance of food for the village.

As the rainy season gets under way in Darfur, UMCOR (United Methodist Committee On Relief) has helped keep hope in the future alive by providing seeds and agricultural tools to displaced families.

9

Gg

Once the grain is grown and harvested, it must be dried then threshed. Threshing means beating the grain so that the grain seeds fall off. The seeds are collected and then ground into meal, which is a course flour used for cooking.

The woman with the basket tosses the grain to separate any remnants of **chaff**, which fly away in the wind. The other two women are grinding. They take turns striking the grain within the hollowed-out log to break it into smaller pieces.

Try grinding your own grain with a mortar and pestle at home!

Grinding grain like sorghum
means pounding with a stick.
It must be crushed and slightly smushed;
the process is not quick.

Humanitarian aid brings needed help
to families in distress.
Those who give also receive
and find that they are blessed.

Hh

The United Nations is often thought to be responsible for taking care of groups of people in crisis around the world. Governments from all around the globe contribute food, money and other items to help areas in which natural disasters and wars have caused trouble. However, we can do more as individuals by personally making an effort to aid another human brother or sister in this world when one is in need.

UMCOR provided the blanket and tarps in this picture.

11

Ii

IDPs are Internally Displaced Persons.

There are millions of men, women, and children now living in displaced person's camps all over Darfur. They are waiting for a safe moment to return to their villages and to have the ability to care for their families once they get home.

Imagine the entire state of Utah displaced and moving on foot into Nevada or Arizona.

Or think about any city with 2.5 million people in it. Imagine someone trying to kill them all because they are different or believe differently.

IDPs have lost their homes,
their towns burned to the ground.
Forced to wander through Darfur
until safe spots are found.

Janjaweed is a funny word.
It's not a plant or flower.
It's a group of men with guns,
making war and taking power.

Jj

This is where a Maali Village used to be, but it was burned to the ground by the Janjaweed.

Janjaweed means "armed horsemen." But sometimes they ride on trucks, too! These are soldiers that may or may not be controlled by the government of the Sudan.

It is not clear who gives them the guns and money to continue hurting the local people.

13

Kk

The children at this school just received new school supplies from UMCOR. This school is coeducational. Some cultures do not believe girls should be educated the same way as boys.

This school meets in a grass building. Some new schools have been built out of stone blocks as well.

What kind of school do you attend? Does it have both boys and girls? Are you happy when you get new school supplies like the children in this picture?

Knowledge is power
for the next generation.
A great education
builds a strong future nation.

UMCOR

Ll

While Arabic is the official language of the Republic of Sudan, several other languages are spoken as well.

Nubian is one of the major tribal languages. Believe it or not, English is also spoken quite a bit.

UMCOR provides chalkboards for schools in Darfur. The writing at the top of the chalkboard in the picture is Arabic.

What language or languages can you speak?

Language is the way we talk
and how we write our words.
The Sudanese officially use
Arabic, I've heard.

Mm

Machines come in all shapes and sizes, but they all help us work faster and easier.

A sewing machine is a **complex** machine. A hoe is a simple machine that a farmer uses. Both are very useful.

Skills training for adults is helping the displaced persons learn to use machines that will help them earn money for their families.

Can you find both a complex machine and a simple machine in your home?

Machines are helpful tools to have when working at a trade. They can help buy food and clothes from money that is paid.

NFIs are a form of aid
  you wouldn't want to eat,
but when it comes to helping out
  they really can't be beat.

Nn

NFIs are Non-Food Items being distributed to IDPs, or Internally Displaced Persons, in the camps.

The farming program is helping feed the IDPs, but they still need things like tarps to keep their homes dry, blankets to keep them warm, and water jugs to carry their water.

Can you find all those items in this picture?

Oo

This native African plant is a crop grown by farmers in Darfur.

Bamia-Bamia is a favorite Sudanese lamb stew that uses okra. You can try some if you follow the recipe on page 38.

Okra was brought to the United States during the time of slavery and is a food often used in southern-style cooking.

Next time you're at the store, look for some okra!

Okra is a silly vegetable,
long and thin and green.
It is a tasty flower pod
used in Sudanese cuisine.

Peanuts pack a protein punch
that grows hearty in Darfur.
These tasty snacks are saving lives
wherever they occur.

Pp

The peanut is actually part of the bean family. It grows underground in its shell with two nuts per shell on average.

Another common name for the peanut is *groundnut*. A silly name for it is *goober*.

The peanut keeps well, can be planted for the next year's crop, and contains lots of energy to fuel a hungry person.

Do you like peanuts? Did you know George Washington Carver, a famous African American, came up with 300 ways to use peanuts?

Qq

The Qoz region of southwestern Sudan is known for its **fertile** qoz sand.

This area contains more reliable sources of water. The sandy soil makes it easier to farm with hand tools.

Gum arabic or *gum acacia* is a sticky substance that comes from the acacia tree. The tree uses the substance to glue its bark back together when it gets cut. The gum is used in soft drinks, marshmallows, watercolor paints, and self-adhesive postage stamps.

Qoz sands in Darfur are good
for growing sticky, gummy trees.
The trees make gum we use in foods.
Pass the gumdrops, please.

Rebuilding is a lot of work.
It takes more than just one.
And when the country is at war
the work is never done.

Rr

Communities must pull together for the task of rebuilding. It takes a lot of time, energy, **commitment**, and resources to construct a building.

We can work with a rebuilding community by providing resources such as materials and money.

This man is building a welcome center for displaced persons that enter the camp. Whenever they can, workers reuse things like wood and bricks.

Do you reuse or recycle things around your home?

21

Ss

Sorghum has been in East Africa for thousands of years. It can survive a long time without water and in high heat.

The sweet variety of sorghum is often squeezed for its sweet syrup.

Sorghum is an ancient grain
that grows well in high heat.
Used for bread, this grain is good
for it is very sweet.

Tools are used
for farming the fields.
Hoeing the ground
grows bigger yields.

Tt

A yield is the amount of food grown in an area.

When one breaks up the weeds and roots and removes stones using a hoe and rake, the ground can provide more nutrients to the plant.

Tools in Darfur are made by local blacksmiths in the city of Al Daein.

Providing work for skilled laborers is like hoeing the economy so that it can grow stronger like the plants in the soft dirt.

23

Uu

Many humanitarian groups are working in the Sudan.

UMCOR is a not-for-profit global humanitarian aid **organization** that works in more than eighty countries worldwide, including the United States. Its mission is to lessen human suffering—whether caused by war, conflict, or natural disaster—with open hearts and minds to all people. It is not a government group; it is funded by donations from ordinary people like you.

UNICEF is another group you may have heard of. This children's aid group is run by the United Nations. Does "Trick-or-Treat for UNICEF" sound familiar?

UMCOR is a group that works with people in Darfur. It sends needed help along with hope to this country caught in war.

Vv

Vehicles are those things that carry something from one place to another.

The most common vehicle in the Sudan is feet!

People also ride horses, donkeys, or camels if they have them. Bicycles provide a faster form of personal **transportation** for those who have to travel longer distances, and they don't have to feed or water a bike!

Vehicles usually have wheels and a seat.
But sometimes a vehicle means using two feet.

25

Ww

Water (H_2O) is essential for life. One can only live three days without water. More importantly one needs CLEAN water. Water can have disease-causing **microorganisms** whether it looks dirty or not. However, at some places in Darfur the water is obviously dirty because animals are drinking it, using it as a toilet, and walking around in it just as the people are!

A *water yard* is a new well that comes from a clean water source and has separate areas for people and animals to get water. One water yard can provide water for 25,000 people and their **livestock** for many years. People often walk for miles with their **jerricans** just to get water.

Water yards pump clean H_2O from wells.
They help stop disease and that's really swell.

X is a symbol for Christ,
God's own son.
The reason this project
was even begun.

Xx

The X is the Greek letter Chi and is the first letter for the word Christ.

The celebration of the birth of Christ is important to Christians.

At Ginghamsburg Church the sentences "Christmas is not your birthday," and "Live simply that others may simply live!" have been used to help people remember the focus of giving a special gift to The Sudan Project.

In 2006, $1,000,000 was raised. Everyone was encouraged to cut back on Christmas gifts and to give at least the same amount to the offering for Darfur.

Yy

Education, skills training, and passing on values are necessary in order to raise the next generation of leaders for a strong country.

The children in this picture received books from UNICEF.

Did you notice how many children were working in all the photographs in this book?

Young people are the Sudan's hope for tomorrow. Investing in them will bring hope over sorrow.

Zz

Some of the tension in the Sudan is centuries old and is between nomadic herding groups and settled farmers. The farmers farm the land, and then a nomadic tribe comes through with its herd, which eats the crops. Conflicts like these, over who controls the land, are difficult to ever resolve.

There are also religious differences since many religions are practiced in the Sudan.

Zaghawa, Masalit, Dinka, and Fur are names of Darfur tribes. This region and its people need the peace that only God prescribes.

29

THE AUTHOR

In her current life, Melissa Leembruggen is a wife and a homeschool mother of three residing in Beavercreek, Ohio, just outside Dayton. Learning new things with the children is a fun benefit of homeschooling. This year she even began taking piano lessons to encourage and motivate the children in their lessons. She believes the Bible is foundational to living an inspired, purposeful life and attends weekly Bible studies to grow in her knowledge and faith. She pursues her professional interests as an author, motivational speaker, and small group trainer/team builder as her time and schedule allow.

Melissa has lived in California, Oregon, Washington, South Carolina, Alabama, and Michigan. She also spent two summer stays in Mexico and Hungary. "Traveling is truly a privilege and joy that enriches my life greatly," reflects the author.

Melissa Leembruggen obtained a Master's Degree in Communication from Auburn University, Class of 1994, where she also worked as Communications Specialist for the Auburn University School of Forestry. She earned her Bachelor's of Science from the University of South Carolina Upstate in International Relations and Speech Communication while working with the Department of Fine Arts and mentor Rachelle Prioleau to found an extracurricular speech and debate program.

THE THANKS

Thank you to the Ginghamsburg Church staff for their support of this project. Thank you to Michelle Scott, Communications Specialist at UMCOR, for a lifeline of photographic images by many talented photographers working with UMCOR and The Sudan Project.

Special thanks to my husband, Oliver, for never laughing at my big ideas and always considering my work equal to his own. Thank you for sharing in the care of our children and for allowing me time to develop my professional skills.

Thank you to Madelyn, Nathaniel, and Jameson for understanding when Mama is working and for loving me through all the moods of the creative, publishing, and promoting processes of this book.

Thank you to my family, The Hagers and The Leembruggens. Thank you to the many friends who encouraged me with homeschooling, motherhood, and professional development: Deanna, Colleen, Tamra, Karene, Jane, Debbie, Janelle, and Joyce.

Thank you to Lyn Chamberlain at Arcadian House for her valuable feedback and encouragement.

GLOSSARY

acclaim—public praise, applause

agricultural—involving farming as a way of life

ancestor—a very distant relative from whom someone is descended, like a great-great-great grandparent, but not a third cousin

border—the outside boundaries (edges) of political places such as a country, state, county, or city

chaff—the dry covering of a grain seed which is separated out in the process of threshing

coeductational—boys and girls together in the same school. Sometimes boys and girls get the same education but are in separate schools. Those are called boys' schools or girls' schools (or single-sex schools).

commitment—doing something or continuing to do something because we have agreed to do it or feel it is important

community—a group of people from the same area or region; a group of people all belonging to the same organization such as a church or a club

complex—something that has two or more parts that go together or work together

continent—a large area of land surrounded on most sides by bodies of water

cuisine—the French word for food

culture—the shared beliefs, customs, practices, and social behaviors of a group of people

displaced—moved from the usual place, especially people who are forced from their homes

economy—how a country takes care of its finances (money) by making and selling goods or services, as well as how much they are buying goods and services

fertile—able to grow and develop

generation—a way of referring to the levels of a family. For example, child to mother is one generation, child to grandmother is two generations, and child to great grandmother is three generations.

government—the group of people that has the power to run a country

humanitarian—a person or persons who help others with health, education, or other problems of injustice

IDPs—Internally Displaced Persons are people who have been forced out of their homes but don't leave their country

jerrican—narrow, flat-sided container for liquids, usually holding about five gallons

livestock—animals raised for use at home or for business, such as for selling milk or wool, for example, cows, sheep, donkeys

microorganisms—living things (such as bacteria) that are too small to see with human eyes

nomads—(adj: nomadic) people that move around from place to place with no one place to call home

nutrients—the vitamins and minerals that are in the soil or in food. Nutrients are needed for growth and health.

nutrition—(adj: nutritional) the way our bodies use foods to help us grow and have good health; nutritional: a way of measuring food and the different kinds of energy and vitamins a food has

organization—a group of people (often lots of people) that work together in a planned way; examples of organizations: governments, churches, sports groups

orphanage—a place for children to live and be cared for when their parents are no longer able to care for them

peninsula—a body of land surrounded on three sides by water

transportation—a means of moving from place to place

tribe—a group of people that have a common background and culture, often used in talking about people who live in an out-of-the-way place

UMCOR—United Methodist Committee on Relief: an organization of the United Methodist Church that uses money donated to help people around the world, including those in the United States, in many ways

UNICEF—United Nations International Children's Emergency Fund: an aid organization sponsored by the United Nations to help the children of the world

vehicle—a machine for transporting persons or things

yield—how much of something is produced, such as the amount of grain someone gets from planting seeds, or the amount of money someone makes from a business

UNIT STUDY PLAN

This study plan can be used for children of almost any age: just pick age-appropriate activities and then have the children complete them at their own level.

Geography
- Draw a map of the Sudan.
  Label the capital, the major rivers, and the major cities.
  Label everything that borders the Republic of Sudan.
  Younger children can trace a map from a book.
- Look up and draw the Sudanese flag.
  Try to find out what each color or item symbolizes.

Science
- Find some simple machines and complex machines.
  How does an inclined plane work?
  How does a lever work?
- Look at microorganisms and discuss why clean water is so important.
- Science experiment—buy three plants of the same type and size.
  Fertilize (feed) and water the first plant,
  only water the second plant,
  and do not feed or water the third plant.
  Make sure they all get the same amount of sunlight.
  Make daily observations about the health of each plant.

History
- Read about the history of the Sudan on *en.wikipedia.org*.
- Make a family tree.
- Read the story in Genesis 9–10 about Noah and his sons.

Culture

- Girls: try wearing a head scarf for a day.
  Boys: try to wear a turban for a day. Visit *www.sikhnet.com/s/tyingturbans*.
- Try the recipe on page 38, or have peanuts for a snack if you aren't allergic to them.
- Middle/high school students: watch *The Lost Boys of Sudan*.
- Visit *music.calabashmusic.com/world/africa/sudan* to sample different Sudanese musical artists.

Community Service

- Contact Catholic Charities, Catholic Social Services, Lutheran Immigration & Refugee Services, or The Salvation Army Immigrant & Refugee Services to see if there are any immigrants in your area that need assistance.
- Pack an Operation Christmas Shoe Box. Some of the boxes go to the Sudan. Visit *www.samaritanspurse.org* for more information.
- Contact Ginghamsburg UMC, UMCOR, UNICEF, Church World Service, or any of the above organizations to see how you may get involved in helping the people of the Sudan.

Art

- Draw your own African cloth pattern. See the pictures on pages 16 and 18.
- Visit *www.languages-of-the-world.us/YourNameIn/Arabic.html* to see your name in Arabic, and then try to write it yourself.
- Build a pyramid out of sugar cubes. How many did it take? (More than you thought?) This activity practices math too!

Language Arts

- Write about three differences between your life and the lives of the children in Darfur.
- Write an e-mail to the author explaining what you liked about this book and what you learned. Use this address: *letters@claybridges.com*.
- Write a paper describing what you think should be done to reduce hunger and poverty in the world.
- Write a poem about life in Darfur. You can send the poem to the author at *letters@claybridges.com*.

NOTE: Websites are constantly changing. Although the websites listed here were checked when this book was published, it is a good idea to preview any website you use with children to make sure it is still active and both age and content appropriate.

QUESTIONS FOR FURTHER DISCUSSION

Is there something you would like to understand better about life in Darfur, Sudan?

What makes you the saddest about the lives of the Sudanese people?

What gives you hope about their lives?

Do you have a favorite picture from this book? What do you like about it?

What kinds of crops do the farmers grow?

What kinds of skills are the adults and older kids learning? Do you think they are learning something that YOU would like to learn?

Would you like to do something personally to help make a difference for kids in Darfur?

HANDS-ON INVOLVEMENT

These suggestions are real things that kids at Ginghamsburg Church (and beyond) have done to raise money to save lives in Darfur, Sudan.

Birthday Party Blessing—Many children have asked their birthday guests to bring money to give to The Sudan Project instead of bringing birthday gifts to their party.

Christmas Gift Take Back—Some children have taken meaningful Christmas Gifts back to the store in order to donate the money to The Sudan Project. (Note: Not all stores refund money for gift items, so this may not work in some cases.)

Sell Something—There are all kinds of things to make and sell, such as decorative note cards, beaded jewelry, baked goods, lemonade, or perennial plants split from starts in your yard.

Do Something—Start an educational and fundraising campaign at your school: run laps/miles (sponsors pledge an amount of money for every lap/mile you run), mow lawns, shovel snow, rake leaves, do laundry or extra chores, or do a read-a-thon (same idea as for running).

Pledge to Pray—Pledge to pray at every meal for those in Darfur that they might have safety, healthy crops, and clean water.

RECIPE

Bamia-Bamia (Sudanese Lamb Stew)

INGREDIENTS:
- 1 pound lamb, cut up for stew
- 1 pound frozen okra
- 16 ounces canned crushed tomatoes
- 4 ounces canned tomato puree
- 1 medium onion, chopped
- 2 cloves garlic, crushed
- ½ teaspoon cumin
- 1 teaspoon coriander
- 8 cups water
- salt and pepper to taste
- 2 tablespoons olive oil

PREPARATION:

In a large saucepan, brown meat with olive oil. Add chopped onion and minced garlic. Add crushed tomatoes, stirring well with meat, garlic and onion. Add seasonings, water, and tomato puree. Stir and combine well. Add okra and bring to a boil. Reduce heat to low and simmer for two hours, or until meat is tender and done. If sauce doesn't thicken, you may add some flour or cornstarch as a thickener.

RESOURCES USED FOR RESEARCH

www.CNN.com

dictionary.reference.com

ginghamsburg.org

www.google.com

www.rhymezone.com

www.sudan.net

ginghamsburg.org/sudan

en.wikipedia.org

news.yahoo.com

gbgm-umc.org/umcor

DOWNLOAD PRINTABLE ACTIVITY PAGES

If you would like downloadable activity pages, they can be found at *www.claybridges.com*.

the sudan PROJECT